TUSCAN

C O O K B O O K

MARY MAW AND RADHA PATTERSON

Illustrated by NEISHA ALLEN

APPLETREE PRESS

First published in 1994 by
The Appletree Press Ltd
19–21 Alfred Street, Belfast BT2 8DL
Tel. +44 232 243074 Fax +44 232 246756
Copyright © 1994 The Appletree Press, Ltd.
Printed in the E.U. All rights reserved.
No part of this publication may be reproduced or
transmitted in any form or by any means, electronic or
mechanical, photocopying, recording or any information
and retrieval system, without permission in writing from
The Appletree Press Ltd.

A Little Tuscan Cookbook

A catalogue record for this book is available
in The British Library.

ISBN 0-86281-505-3

9 8 7 6 5 4 3 2 1

Introduction

Probably the best known of all Italian regions, Tuscany is famed for the glorious Renaissance art and architecture of its towns and cities and the beauty of its villages and countryside. Tuscan wines and olive oil are among the finest produced in Italy and Tuscan food is no less excellent. Noted for its simplicity and purity, the region's cooking stems from ancient rural traditions yet has enormous appeal for today's health-conscious cook. Meats in a Tuscan kitchen are grilled or roasted; vegetables are plainly cooked or eaten raw. Bread is consumed in great quantities, puddings are reserved for special occasions, and butter and cream are not much used. Olive oil is the major distinctive ingredient in Tuscan cooking. Rosemary and garlic provide two other typical flavours. Rice and pasta play only minor roles in the traditional Tuscan diet and meals are usually begun with a soup. Pulses in the form of cannellini beans and chick peas are popular hence the Tuscans' nickname I *Mangiafagioli* – the bean eaters! Not much cheese is made in the region but, of Italy's ewe's milk cheeses, *Pecorino Toscano* is considered one of the finest.

The recipes chosen to represent Tuscan cooking do not require obscure ingredients or special equipment. They do call for, above all else, the best quality (preferably Tuscan) olive oil and the freshest produce available. Equipped with these we hope our selection will allow you to recreate the flavours of Tuscany in your own kitchen and inspire you to delve further into the delights of Tuscan cooking.

A note on measures
Metric, imperial and volume measurements are given for all recipes. For best results use one set only. Recipes are for four unless otherwise indicated.

3

Pinzimonio

A bowl of virgin olive oil into which crunchy vegetables are dipped and then eaten is the inspiration for this simple dish. In this version finely chopped fennel, rosemary, garlic and chilli, flavours redolent of Tuscan cooking, are added to the olive oil. Served with good bread, *Pinzimonio* is a delightful introduction to Tuscan food.

$^1/_2$ *large bulb of fennel*
1 small dried chilli
$^1/_2$ *clove of garlic*
sprig of fresh rosemary
$^1/_4$ *pt/125ml/$^1/_2$ cup extra-virgin olive oil*
salt and freshly ground black pepper

Chop the fennel, garlic, chilli and rosemary very finely (the Italian implement called *mezzaluna* is most effective). Add to the olive oil, mix well, and season with salt and pepper to taste. Leave for several hours to allow flavours to mingle. Serve with slices of crusty bread or Tuscan *schiacciata* (see p. 11).

Bruschetta al Pomodoro

Ripe tomatoes, extra-virgin olive oil and bread are the ingredients for these canapés served in *trattorie* all over Tuscany. Alas, tomatoes available elsewhere are not always as flavoursome as those grown in central Italy. A few drops of balsamic vinegar, though not strictly Tuscan can, however, enliven dull tomatoes and dried oregano is an acceptable substitute when fresh basil is not available.

1 lb/550g tomatoes
6 tbsp extra-virgin olive oil
a few leaves of basil torn into small pieces,
or a large pinch of dried oregano
a few drops of balsamic vinegar
salt and freshly ground black pepper
12 slices of crusty French or Italian-style bread
1 clove of garlic, peeled
(makes 12)

Using a swivel-action potato peeler remove the skin from the tomatoes with a sawing motion. Quarter them, remove the core and seeds and chop them into small pieces. Toss with half the olive oil, the basil or oregano, a few drops of balsamic vinegar, salt and pepper. Brush the bread with the remaining olive oil, rub with the garlic clove and toast under a hot grill until golden brown. Top with the tomato mixture and serve at once.

Crostini di Fegatini

These delicious Tuscan *crostini* make ideal pre-dinner canapés. The chicken mixture should be eaten slightly warm and used within 24 hours.

---

2 tbsp olive oil
1oz/25g butter
1 small onion, finely chopped
1 stick of celery, finely chopped
½ carrot, finely chopped
8oz/225g chicken livers, cleaned and chopped into small pieces
3 tbsp dry white wine
2 anchovy fillets, finely chopped

1 tbsp capers, finely chopped
salt and freshly ground black pepper
½ large French baguette or Italian-style country loaf cut into 16 slices approximately ¾ in/2 cm thick
4 tbsp olive oil
16 gherkins

(makes 16)

Place the olive oil and half the butter in a saucepan. Melt the butter and add the finely chopped onion, celery and carrot. Cook for 10–15 minutes, stirring frequently. When the vegetables are soft, lower the heat and add the chicken livers. Cook for a few minutes until the livers turn brown. Raise the heat, add the white wine and simmer until it evaporates. Salt to taste, cover the pan and cook at low heat for 10–15 minutes. Add the anchovies, capers, pepper and the remaining butter. Blend the mixture in a food processor briefly or chop it by hand. It should retain a granular consistency.

To make the *crostini*, brush the slices of bread with the olive oil and toast under a hot grill until golden brown. Top each slice with the chicken liver mixture and garnish with a gherkin. Serve at once.

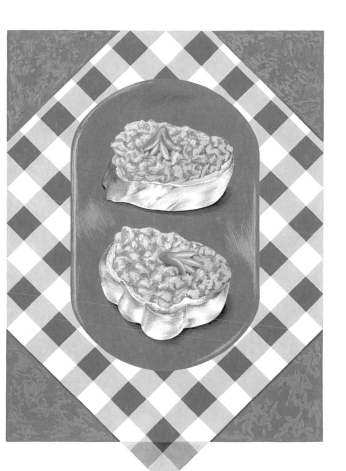

Schiacciata

Bread is a vital part of Tuscan cuisine. It is eaten not only as an accompaniment to meals but as an ingredient in soups and salads. *Schiacciata* (which means flat bread) is Tuscany's version of *focaccia*. Easy to make and very flavoursome, it can be filled to make delicious sandwiches, covered with a topping like a pizza, or simply enjoyed with antipasto or soup.

1 ½ lbs/540g/6 ⅓ cup strong white flour	3 tbsp olive oil
½oz/10g active dried yeast granules	¾ pt/425ml/2 cups hand-hot water
2 tsp salt	olive oil
½oz/10g sugar	sea salt
	fresh or dried rosemary

Sift the flour and salt into a bowl. In a separate bowl, mix the yeast and sugar with ¼ pt/125ml/½ cup of the water. Make a well in the centre of the flour. When the yeast has dissolved and begins to fizz, add the rest of the water and the olive oil and pour this mixture gradually into the flour. Mix the dough until it is soft and sticky and then turn it onto a floured surface. Cover and allow it to rest for 5 minutes. The dough should then be kneaded for 10 minutes until smooth and springy to the touch. Place the dough in a bowl, cover with cling film and leave to rise in a warm place for about 2 hours until it has doubled in size. Oil an oven sheet and, when the dough has risen, knead it lightly again and form into two 12 inch/30 cm circles. Put the circles on the baking sheet and leave to rise again for about 20 minutes. Meanwhile, pre-heat the oven to gas mark 7, 425°F, 220°C. When the bread has risen another ½ inch / 1 cm or so, press fingers into the surface to create little dimples. Brush the top of the bread liberally with olive oil and sprinkle with sea salt and rosemary. Bake for 15 minutes and then reduce heat to gas mark 6, 400°F, 200°C and bake for a further 5–10 minutes. When the bread is golden brown, remove it from the oven and place on a wire rack. Using your fingers, gently spread olive oil over the surface of the bread and allow to cool before serving.

Polpette

Polpette (meatballs) are found all over Italy but are thought to have originated in Tuscany. They can be made with almost any type of cooked meat, minced veal and pork being the most commonly used. Often *prosciutto* is combined with the meat but in this recipe mortadella sausage is used to give delicious results. Served with a salad, *polpette* make a splendid light lunch. They are also excellent as pre-dinner canapés.

6oz/180g cooked breast of chicken	4oz/100g boiled potato, mashed
3oz/90g mortadella sausage	salt and pepper
1 clove garlic, finely chopped	1 egg, beaten
2oz/50g grated Parmesan cheese	breadcrumbs
1 tbsp parsley, finely chopped	sunflower or arachide oil for frying
	lemon wedges
(makes 12–16)	

Put the cooked breast of chicken and the mortadella sausage in a food processor and blend for a couple of minutes. Empty into a bowl and combine with the chopped garlic, Parmesan cheese, parsley and the mashed potato. Season with salt and pepper and bind the paste with the beaten egg. Shape the mixture into small

balls or sausage shapes, roll in the breadcrumbs and fry in the hot oil until crisp and golden. Drain on kitchen paper and serve immediately with wedges of lemon.

Panzanella

This rustic salad was orginally made with bread soaked in water. In these more affluent times, cubes of bread toasted in olive oil make this classic Tuscan dish a sophisticated first course or light lunch.

Croutons

4oz/100g crusty French or Italian-style bread	2 tbsp extra-virgin olive oil salt

---

Cube the bread into 1 inch / 2 cm pieces. Place the cubes of bread on a large baking tray and drizzle the olive oil over them, ensuring they are well covered. Sprinkle lightly with salt. Pre-heat the oven to gas mark 6, 400°F, 200°C and bake the croutons until crisp and brown (10–15 minutes). Be vigilant as they burn easily.

Panzanella

1/2 clove garlic	1/2 red onion, finely sliced
1 tbsp capers	1 yellow pepper, seeds and pulpy
2 flat anchovy fillets	core removed, and cut into
5 tbsp extra-virgin olive oil	2 in/5 cm cubes
salt and freshly ground	1/2 cucumber, halved length-
black pepper	ways and cut into slices
1 tbsp red wine vinegar	10 basil leaves, torn into small
1 quantity of croutons	pieces
3 firm, ripe tomatoes, seeded and cut into 1 in/2 cm strips	

To make the dressing, combine the garlic, capers, anchovies, oil, salt and vinegar in a food processor and blend to a smooth consistency. Place the croutons, cut up vegetables and basil leaves in a bowl and pour over the dressing. Add several gridings of black pepper, toss thoroughly and serve at once.

Tonno e Fagioli

This popular dish combines Tuscany's beloved beans with tinned tuna fish to produce a substantial salad suitable for a first course or light lunch. Tinned cannellini beans may be used but the texture and flavour of cooked dried beans is vastly superior.

14oz/400g dried cannellini beans	juice of $^1/_2$ a lemon
1 onion, peeled	3 6oz/160g tins of tuna in
1 bay leaf	olive oil
salt and freshly ground	$^1/_2$ red onion, cut into thin slices
black pepper	small bunch of parsley,
$^1/_4$ pt/125ml/$^2/_3$ cup olive oil	finely chopped

Soak the cannellini beans in cold water for 5–6 hours or overnight. Discard the soaking water and place in large saucepan together with onion and bay leaf. Cover with water and bring to the boil. Remove any scum that floats to the surface. Reduce to a simmer, cover and cook for 40–60 minutes. The cooking time depends on the age of the beans so test them every now and again. Add salt to taste at the end of the cooking time.

When the beans are tender, but not mushy, drain them and discard the onion and the bay leaf. While still warm, put the beans into a large bowl and dress with the olive oil, salt, pepper and the

lemon juice. Add the drained tuna, using a fork to break it into chunks, and the finely sliced onion. Toss the ingredients to mix well, garnish with chopped parsley and serve.

Passata di Peperone

Roasted yellow pepper soup is based on a traditional Tuscan country recipe. It is ideal with thick, crusty bread which has been brushed with extra-virgin olive oil and then grilled.

2lb 2oz/1 kg yellow peppers
1 carrot, finely chopped
1 stick celery, finely chopped
1 medium onion, finely chopped
2 medium potatoes, peeled and diced
2 tbsp olive oil
1³/₄ pt/1 lt/4¹/₂ cups chicken stock
salt and freshly ground black pepper

First roast the peppers by putting them under a hot grill until the skin is blistered all over. Cool them, and peel off the charred skin. De-seed, cut into strips and set aside.

Put the olive oil into a deep saucepan and add the chopped onion, carrot and celery. Cook until the vegetables soften. Add the yellow peppers and cook for a further 10 minutes, then add the potatoes and chicken stock. Bring to the boil, lower heat and simmer for 30 minutes. Purée the vegetables and add salt and pepper to taste. Drizzle some olive oil on to the soup and serve at once.

Minestra di Pasta e Ceci

This soup is found all over central Italy. There are many recipes for it, but this is a typically Tuscan version. It is a very rich soup, and should be served in small quantities.

8oz/200g/1 cup chick peas
3 tbsp extra-virgin olive oil
1 medium onion, peeled and chopped
1 medium carrot, diced
1 stick celery, chopped
3 cloves of garlic, crushed
3 pt/1.5 lt/8 cups water
3oz/75g/¹⁄₂ cup pasta such as stelline or tiny macaroni
salt and freshly ground black pepper
chilli-flavoured olive oil (optional)

Place the chick peas in a bowl and pour boiling water over them. Leave to soak for one hour. Put oil in large saucepan and add chopped vegetables and garlic. Cook for about 10 minutes over a moderate heat until soft. Add the drained chick peas and stir to coat with oil. Pour in the water, cover and bring to a simmer. Cook until chick-peas are tender (1–2 hours). Be sure to stir the soup from time to time to prevent the vegetables from sticking. When the chick peas are tender, purée them. The soup should be creamy in texture but not entirely smooth. Add the pasta, salt and black pepper and cook for a further 10 minutes, stirring frequently. A few drops of olive oil flavoured with chilli greatly enlivens this soup.

Pappa al Pomodoro

A traditional Tuscan dish, this dense, flavoursome soup is found all over the region. Made with plenty of garlic, ripe tomatoes, extra-virgin olive oil and fresh basil, it is the perfect first course on a summer evening.

---

8 fl oz/200ml/1 cup extra-virgin olive oil
8 cloves of garlic, finely chopped
10 leaves of basil – more if you prefer
1 lb/500g tomatoes, peeled and chopped
1 lb/500g country-style bread (1–2 days old) torn into small pieces
2 medium onions, finely sliced
1 3/4 pt/1 lt/4 1/2 cups vegetable stock
2 tsp sugar
4 tbsp tomato paste
salt and pepper to taste
1 crushed dried red chilli pepper

Heat the oil in a deep saucepan and fry the onion until it is soft, but not brown. Add the sugar and cook for 5 minutes. Put in the garlic and chilli pepper . When these soften (about 10 minutes), add the tomatoes, the tomato paste and the basil leaves and cook for a further 10 minutes. Put in the stock and the seasoning. After the mixture has come to the boil, add the bread. Cook for 40 minutes over a low heat, stirring from time to time. Mix well before serving and pour on some olive oil. Serve warm or at room temperature, garnished with basil leaves.

Pinci con Sugo di Salsiccia

Fresh pasta is not traditionally part of Tuscan cooking. In the Siena area, however, *pinci* (a kind of handmade spaghetti) is found. Not a dish for those in a hurry as each strand of pasta is rolled by hand, *pinci* is none the less worth the effort and makes the perfect partner for a robust sauce made with meaty Italian sausage.

Pinci

1 lb/500g/3 cups strong white flour	1 tbsp olive oil
pinch of salt	8–12 fl oz/200–300ml/ 1–1 1/2 cups cold water

Place the flour and salt in a mound on a flat surface and make a well in the centre. Pour on some of the water and draw in the flour from the edge. Repeat this process until the dough is firm but sticky, using more water if necessary. Add the olive oil and knead the dough for 2–3 minutes until smooth and springy to the touch. Flatten the dough to a thickness of 1/2 inch / 1 cm. Cut it into 1/2 inch / 1 cm strips and then into 1/2 inch / 1 cm cubes. Take each cube and using finger and thumb flatten out to about 3 inch / 7 cm length. Then, using the palms of the hand, roll the length of the pasta dough into rounded strips about 8–9 inches / 21 cm long. Place on cotton towels until ready to use. To cook, bring a large saucepan of water to the boil. Add the *pinci* and boil for 1–3 minutes until *al dente*.

Sauce

1 tbsp extra-virgin olive oil	salt and freshly ground black pepper
2 cloves of garlic, finely chopped	
8oz/200g meaty sausages (preferably Italian), skinned	2oz/50g freshly grated Parmesan cheese

PINCI

14oz/400g tin Italian tomatoes,
chopped

Put the oil and garlic into a sauté pan and cook until the garlic is coloured. Add the sausages, using a fork to break them up. Cook until the sausages are well browned. Add the tomatoes and simmer until they separate from the oil. Season with salt and pepper and use the sauce to dress the *pinci*. Serve with the grated Parmesan cheese.

Penne all' Arrabiata

The dried pasta shape most characteristic of the Tuscan region is *penne*, so-called because of its quill-like shape. The sauce is described as *arrabiata* which means angry because it is "enraged" with chilli, a spice commonly used in the area but confusingly called *zenzero*, the name for ginger elsewhere in Italy.

---

2 tbsp extra-virgin olive oil
2 cloves of garlic, finely chopped
1 dried chilli pepper, crushed
2oz/50g pancetta, cut into
narrow strips
2 14oz/400g tins of tomatoes,
chopped

1 lb/500g penne
few leaves of basil torn into
small pieces
1oz/25g Parmesan cheese, grated
1oz/25g pecorino cheese, grated

Put the olive oil in a large sauté pan and add the garlic and chilli. When the garlic begins to colour, add the *pancetta* and fry until it is brown but not crisp. Put in the chopped tomatoes and simmer for about half an hour until they separate from the oil. Cook the *penne* in a large saucepan of salted boiling water until *al dente*. Add the basil to the sauce and cook for a few more minutes. Drain the pasta, add the sauce and the cheeses and serve at once.

Manzo Brasato al Chianti

This delicious recipe for beef cooked in wine is found all over Italy and dates as far back as the sixteenth century. Chianti Classico, the great wine of the region south of Florence, is used here to give the meat its excellent flavour.

2lb 2oz/1 kg topside of beef, all in one piece
2oz/25g pancetta
1 carrot, diced
1 stick celery, diced
1 medium onion, thinly sliced
4 fat cloves of garlic cut in to slivers
3 tbsp olive oil
2 wine glasses Chianti or other red wine
salt and freshly ground black pepper

With a sharp knife make several slits in the beef and insert a sliver of garlic and a sliver of *pancetta* into each slit. Put the olive oil into a large casserole and brown the beef in it. Add the chopped vegetables and let them soften. Pour in the wine and the seasoning and bring to the boil. Lower the heat and cover. The beef should simmer for 3–4 hours and the heat should be so low that barely a bubble breaks the surface. At the end of the cooking time, remove the meat, cut it into thick slices, spoon the sauce over them and serve at once.

Bistecca alla Fiorentina

One of the best known dishes of Tuscany is the Florentine *bistecca* – a thick T-bone steak which is lightly grilled over charcoal and eaten *al sangue* (very rare). The success of this dish depends on the quality of the meat and Tuscan beef is considered to be particularly fine. It can be cooked either on a barbecue or a domestic grill.

2 very large T-bone steaks – 1 1/2 lb/750g each
1 tbsp olive oil
salt and freshly ground black pepper

Heat the grill and, when very hot, lay the steaks side by side under it. Cook for 4 minutes or until the meat darkens. Turn the steaks over and season with salt and black pepper and cook the second side for a further 4 minutes. If you do not like the meat rare, cook for a further 2 minutes. Brush the steaks with olive oil and serve immediately.

Agnello col Olive Nere

This dish originates from Lucca – an area famous for its olives – and variations are found all over Tuscany. This recipe includes dried red chilli pepper – a flavour typical of Tuscan cooking.

---

3 tbsp oil
2 sprigs fresh rosemary
2 cloves garlic, finely chopped
2lb 2oz/1 kg shoulder of lamb, cubed
2 wine glasses of dry white wine
6 large ripe tomatoes, peeled and chopped
1 tbsp of grated lemon rind
1 dried red chilli pepper
4oz/125g of pitted black olives
salt and freshly ground black pepper

Heat the oil in a wide pan, add the garlic and rosemary, and cook until the garlic colours. Put in the cubes of lamb and turn them in the hot oil until they brown. Pour in the wine and when it has reduced to half, add the tomatoes, the lemon rind and the chilli pepper. Cover and cook over a low heat for about 20 minutes. Add the olives, cover again and cook for a further hour or so, stirring from time to time to prevent the meat from sticking. Add a little water if the stew gets too dry. At the end of the cooking time, the meat should be moist and tender.

Arista alla Fiorentina

According to legend, the Greek bishops who served this dish at an ecumenical council held in Florence in 1430 pronounced it *aristos*, the Greek word for "best". This roast loin of pork is indeed exceedingly good.

3lb/1.5 kg boneless loin of pork with a good covering of fat
4 cloves of garlic, peeled
6 sage leaves
leaves from 2 sprigs of rosemary
3 tbsp olive oil
salt and freshly ground black pepper

Preheat the oven to gas mark 6, 400°F, 200°C. Combine the oil, garlic, herbs and seasoning in a food processor and blend together. Rub the oil and herb mixture over the pork, making incisions in the fat and pushing the mixture into them. Roll the pork up tightly and tie at intervals with string. Roast for 1½–2 hours on a wire rack until the juices run clear. Carve into slices and serve at once.

Pollo al Diavolo

The best free-range Italian chickens are said to come from Tuscany and Tuscan cooks are regarded as experts at preparing delicious chicken dishes. Like so much Tuscan food this dish is simplicity itself but calls for a top quality free-range bird. It is best barbecued, but can be cooked very successfully under a domestic grill.

3–3¹/₂ lb/1.5 kg chicken
olive oil
salt and freshly ground black pepper
¹/₂ dried red chilli pepper (crushed)
juice of 1 lemon

Split the chicken open along the breast and flatten as much as possible. Cover with a mixture of olive oil, lemon juice, crushed chilli, salt and pepper. Leave to marinate for at least one hour. Barbecue or grill for 30–40 minutes, brushing occasionally with the marinade until the juices from the thigh run clear.

Petti di Pollo con Salsa di Dragoncello

Tarragon is not a herb usually associated with Italian cooking but in the area around Siena it appears in some dishes – hence its other name, *erba di Siena*. The sauce in this recipe more usually accompanies boiled meats but is delicious served with chicken.

4 chicken breasts, boned and skinned
1 tbsp flour
salt and freshly ground black pepper
2oz/50g butter

Dust the chicken breasts with the flour, salt and pepper. Heat the butter in a large frying pan and when it has melted, add the chicken breasts and fry on both sides until brown. Reduce heat, cover the pan and cook the breasts for a further 15–20 minutes.

Sauce
1½oz/40g fresh white breadcrumbs
1 clove of garlic, finely chopped
large bunch of tarragon, finely chopped
2 tbsp parsley, finely chopped
1 hard-boiled egg yolk, well mashed
salt and freshly ground black pepper
¼ pt/125ml extra-virgin olive oil
1 tbsp red wine vinegar

Soak the breadcrumbs in water for 5 minutes. Combine the garlic, parsley and tarragon in a bowl. Squeeze the water out of the breadcrumbs and add to the chopped herbs along with the egg yolk, salt and pepper. Slowly drizzle the olive oil onto this mixture, stirring constantly, until the sauce is smooth and even. Refrigerate for an hour or so, add the vinegar and serve the sauce with the chicken.

Sogliole alla Fiorentina

Spinach features prominently in the cooking of Tuscany and the word "Florentine" is now a standard culinary term describing eggs or fish served on a bed of spinach. This classic recipe calls for sole, but plaice or other white fish are just as suitable.

2lb 2oz/1 kg fresh spinach, or 1 lb/500g frozen spinach, thawed
5oz/125g butter
pinch of grated nutmeg
8 fillets of sole
1 glass dry white wine
2oz/50g plain flour
17 fl oz/500ml/2 cups hot milk
3oz/90g grated Parmesan cheese
salt and freshly ground black pepper

Pre-heat the oven to gas mark 6, 400°F, 200°C. If you are using fresh spinach, wash the leaves thoroughly and place in a saucepan with 1oz/25g of the butter. Cook briefly until the leaves wilt. Season with salt, pepper and grated nutmeg. If you are using frozen spinach, thaw in a saucepan over moderate heat, drain and squeeze out all the moisture. Add 1oz/25g butter and season as above.

Melt 2oz/50g butter in a frying pan and add the wine. Warm through for a few minutes and then add the sole. Cook the sole fillets for about 7 minutes, set aside and boil the wine briskly until it has reduced by half. Melt the remaining butter in a small saucepan, add the flour and mix thoroughly to form a smooth *roux*. Gradually add the hot milk, stirring as you do and let the mixture thicken. Season with salt and pepper and more nutmeg. Put in the

reduced wine mixture and stir to amalgamate. Grease an ovenproof gratin dish and cover the base with the spinach. Lay the fish on top and coat with the sauce. Sprinkle with the Parmesan cheese and bake for 15–20 minutes until a golden crust has formed over the top.

Trote alla Griglia

The many rivers which flow through the Tuscan countryside ensure a rich supply of freshwater fish in inland areas. Most popular is trout, and in this recipe it is served grilled in the Tuscan fashion.

---

4 brown or rainbow trout, cleaned but with heads left on
4oz/100g white breadcrumbs
2 cloves of garlic, finely chopped
few leaves of rosemary, finely chopped
bunch of parsley, finely chopped
salt and freshly ground black pepper
extra-virgin olive oil

Briefly soak the breadcrumbs in water and then squeeze them dry. Combine the breadcrumbs, garlic, rosemary, parsley, salt, pepper and a little olive oil in a food processor and mix to a paste-like consistency. Wash and dry the cavities of the trout and stuff with this mixture. Close with toothpicks. Brush the fish with olive oil and sprinkle with salt. Cook on a barbecue or under a hot grill, basting the trout with the olive oil from time to time.

Patate al Forno

Although not an everyday food, potatoes do feature in northern Italian cooking. This recipe combines the basic Tuscan ingredients of olive oil, rosemary and garlic with potatoes to produce a dish which is the perfect partner for the region's grilled and roast meats.

---

1 1/2 lb/750g small new potatoes
2 cloves of garlic, peeled
6 tbsp olive oil
salt and freshly ground black pepper
2 sprigs of rosemary

Pre-heat the oven to gas mark 6, 400°F, 200°C. Wash the potatoes and boil until just tender and then drain. Put the oil, rosemary and garlic into a baking dish and warm in oven for 5 minutes. Add the potatoes, a generous sprinkling of salt and some pepper. Bake for 20–30 minutes, turning from time to time until the skins are golden brown.

Piselli alla Toscana

Garden peas are thought to have been developed in Italy in the sixteenth century and it is said they were one of Catherine de Medici's favourite foods. Unless you grow your own, fresh garden peas are not easily found. This Tuscan recipe, however, turns even the humble frozen pea into something special.

---

2 lb 2oz/1 kg garden peas, shelled or
10oz/285g frozen peas, defrosted
2 cloves garlic, peeled
2 tbsp extra-virgin olive oil
2 tbsp pancetta or prosciutto, finely chopped
2 tbsp parsley, finely chopped
salt and freshly ground black pepper

Sauté the garlic in the olive oil until golden brown and then remove from the saucepan. Add the *pancetta* and cook for a few minutes. Pour in the peas and turn them in the oil. Put in the parsley, salt and pepper to taste. If using fresh peas, add a little water. Reduce the heat and cook the peas until tender – 15–30 minutes if fresh, 5 minutes if frozen.

Fagioli a l'Ucelletto

Tuscans are sometimes described as *I Mangiafagioli* – bean eaters – because of their fondness for beans. Cannellini are the variety most frequently used in this typically Tuscan recipe which makes an ideal companion to the roast loin of pork.

---

1 lb/500g/2 cups cannellini beans soaked
for 5-6 hours or overnight
1 onion, peeled
2 sprigs of sage
6 tbsp olive oil
2 cloves of garlic, peeled
14oz/400g tin of tomatoes
salt and freshly ground black pepper

Drain the beans and put them in a large saucepan. Cover with cold water and bring to the boil. Cook for 3 minutes. Drain and rinse the beans and return to the pan with the onion. Cover with cold water and return to the boil. Let the beans simmer until tender – about 40 minutes – 1 hour. Five minutes or so before the end of cooking, add salt to taste, drain the beans and discard the onion. Heat the oil together with the sage leaves and garlic. Add the tomatoes and simmer for 10 minutes and then add the beans. Season with salt and pepper and simmer for another 15–20 minutes.

Zucchini al Forno

Courgettes are popular throughout Italy and courgette fields in bloom are a glorious sight in the Tuscan countryside.

This dish makes a wonderful light summer lunch and goes very well with *insalata verde* and crusty bread. It is good served hot or cold.

---

4 large or 8 small courgettes
2–3 tbsp plain flour
7 fl oz/200ml/³/₄ cup vegetable oil
8 eggs beaten
4 tbsp milk
salt and freshy ground black pepper
2 tbsp roughly torn fresh basil leaves
4oz/100g freshly grated Parmesan cheese
3 tbsp fresh white breadcrumbs

Top and tail the courgettes and then cut lengthways into ¹/₂ inch / 1 cm slices. Coat the slices lightly in the flour and fry in hot oil until they are crisp and golden. Drain on kitchen paper. Oil a circular ovenproof dish and arrange the courgette slices like the spokes of a wheel. Beat together the eggs, milk, salt, pepper and half the cheese. Add the basil leaves and pour this mixture over the courgettes. Sprinkle the breadcrumbs and the remaining parmesan cheese over the top. Pre-heat the oven to gas mark 5, 375°F, 190°C. Bake the courgettes in the oven for about 15–20 minutes until the top is just firm to the touch.

Insalata Verde

A green salad served after the second course is an essential part of a Tuscan meal. The components of the salad will change according to seasonal availability of lettuces, radicchio, rocket or other green leaves, but the dressing never varies.

A perfectly dressed salad requires salt, extra-virgin Tuscan olive oil and good quality wine vinegar. Marcella Hazan in *The Essentials of Classic Italian Cooking* quotes a proverb which says four persons are required for a good salad: a judicious one for the salt, a prodigal one for the olive oil, a stingy one for the vinegar and a patient one to toss. These ingredients are never mixed in advance but added at the table in the order given and the salad is served at once.

Ricotta al Caffe

Ricotta, a soft cheese made from whey, is produced throughout Italy. It is used in puddings, as a filling for pasta and savoury tarts or eaten on its own. This Tuscan recipe, originally a *merenda* or mid-morning dish, makes a delicious dessert.

***

12oz/350g ricotta
5oz/150g icing sugar
3 tbsp strong black coffee
2 tbsp brandy or other spirits to taste
grated chocolate or cocoa powder

***

Combine the *ricotta*, icing sugar, coffee and brandy in a food processor and blend briefly. Leave for an hour or so to allow the

flavours to develop. To serve, line four ramekin dishes with cling film and fill with the *ricotta* cream. Unmould on to dessert plates. Sprinkle each pudding with grated chocolate or cocoa powder and serve at once.

Torta a Riso

Risotto does not feature in traditional Tuscan cooking, but arborio rice is used to make cakes and puddings. This rice cake is best made one day in advance and keeps well if it is wrapped in tin foil and stored in a cool place. *Amaretti* are crispy, almond-flavoured biscuits. In this recipe they make a happy alternative to plain breadcrumbs.

1¼ pt/750ml full-cream milk
strip of lemon peel
6oz/180g caster sugar
few drops of vanilla essence or a piece of vanilla pod
4 eggs separated
a pinch of salt
5oz/125g arborio rice
2 tbsp brandy
2oz/50g candied peel, finely chopped
butter for greasing cake tin
2 pairs amaretti biscuits crushed
icing sugar for dusting

Place milk, lemon peel, caster sugar, vanilla and salt in a saucepan. Bring to the boil and add the rice. Cook on a low heat until the rice has absorbed all the milk stirring from time to time. Allow to cool, remove lemon peel and, if using, the vanilla pod. Mix in egg yolks, candied peel and brandy. Whisk egg whites until stiff and fold into the rice mixture. Pre-heat oven to gas mark 4, 350°F, 180°C. Grease an 8-inch spring-form tin with butter and sprinkle the bottom and sides with *amaretti* crumbs. Spoon in rice mixture and bake for 45 minutes–1 hour. Allow cake to cool in the tin. When cold, unmould and store in a cool place for 24 hours. Before serving, dust with icing sugar. A fruit purée, such as raspberry or apricot, goes very well with this pudding.

Zuccotto

A speciality of Florence, this dome-shaped pudding may have been inspired by the great cupola of the Duomo which dominates the skyline of the city. Stunning to look at and wickedly rich, it is a spectacular dessert.

19oz/540g rectangular madeira or sponge cake
3oz/75g glacé fruits, chopped into small pieces
3 tbsp cointreau, 3 tbsp brandy (mixed together)
25 fl oz/750ml/3$^{1}/_{3}$ cups double cream
6oz/175g dark chocolate
2oz/50g icing sugar

Line a 2 pint / 1.1 litre bowl with cling film. Cut the cake lengthwise into slices about $^{1}/_{4}$ inch / $^{1}/_{2}$ cm thick and line the bowl with them, working as neatly as possible, filling all gaps. Sprinkle the cake with the cointreau and brandy mixture. Chop 4oz/110g of the chocolate into small pieces. Whip half the cream and the icing sugar together until stiff and add the glacé fruits and half the chopped chocolate.

56

Spread half this mixture over the cake leaving a well in the centre.
Melt the rest of the chopped chocolate in a bowl over simmering
water, fold it into the remaining cream and fruit mixture and fill the
hollow in the centre of the pudding. Use the rest of the cake to
make a lid for the pudding. Cover with cling film and refrigerate
overnight. Before serving, unmould the pudding onto a plate.
Whip the remaining cream until stiff. Melt the remaining 2 oz of
the chocolate and mix with ¾ of the cream. Spread the chocolate
cream over the pudding, smoothing with a palette knife as you go
along. Put the remaining cream into a piping bag and pipe five lines
of cream from the top of the pudding to the base at equal intervals.
Keep refrigerated until served.

Pere e Pecorino

Pecorino is an ewe's milk cheese produced all over central and
southern Italy. Those made in Tuscany are held by many to be the
most superior of the pecorinos. The cheese made in the area south
of Siena known as *pecorino della crete senesi* is highly regarded.
Pecorino from the Pienza area is also considered excellent. Tuscan
pecorino can be eaten when it is two weeks old or when aged for
six months. Traditionally, it is enjoyed at the end of a meal with
fresh broad beans when they are in season. It is also delicious
served with juicy ripe pears whose flavour complements very well
the piquancy of the pecorino.

Index

Agnello col Olive Nere 32
Arista alla Fiorentina 35

Bistecca alla Fiorentina 31
Bruschetta al Pomodoro 7

Crostini di Fegatini 8

Fagioli a l'Ucelletto 48

Insalata Verde 52

Manzo Brasato al Chianti 28
Minestra di Pasta e Ceci 20

Panzanella 15
Pappa al Pomodoro 23
Passata di Peperone 19
Patate al Forno 44
Penne all' Arrabiata 27

Pere e Pecorino 59
Pette di Pollo con Salsa di
    Dragoncello 36
Pinci con Sugo di Salsiccia 24
Pinzimonio 4
Piselli alla Toscana 47
Pollo al Diavolo 36
Polpette 12

Ricotta al Caffe 52

Schiacciata 11
Sogliole all Fiorentina 40

Tonno e Fagioli 16
Torta a Riso 55
Trote all Griglia 43

Zucchini al Forno 51
Zuccotto 56